Tinikling

Tinikling
Karl Riordan

Smokestack Books
1 Lake Terrace,
Grewelthorpe,
Ripon
HG4 3BU
e-mail: info@smokestack-books.co.uk

www.smokestack-books.co.uk

Text copyright 2023,
Karl Riordan,
all rights reserved.

ISBN 9781739173050

Smokestack Books is represented
by Inpress Ltd

for Jeni
in solidarity with the OFWs
separated from their families.

Contents

Tatay Nick's	11
Cosmonaut	13
Boy Nita's	15
Coming to the fence	16
Peeling pomelo	17
Wake	18
'Equalizer'	19
The Tubig Man	20
Daredevil	21
Yellow Brick Road	22
Majorettes	23
The men who sleep in trucks	24
The Scaffolders' Daytime Disco	25
Mangos	27
Pagmamaneho sa timog	28
How to bring down a chimney stack	30
Kevin	31
Gym-Rat	32
Mulligan Stew	33
Silodrome	34
Miriam	35
The Shed	36
Drawing a diagram for my mother	37
French Lesson	38
One at a time...	39
Sirens	40
Northern Soul	41
The Robin	42
The Ticklish Butcher	43
Club trip	44
The Rowan Tree	45
Music row	46
Tommy Murray's brolly	47

Joey	48
The Mirror Man	49
Malaya Never Again	50
The Snog	51
Jubilee	52
Musculoskeletal Imaging	53
Afore ye go	54
Hail Mary	55
Too daft to laugh at	56
Lolo in Levi's	57
Waiting for Arthur	58
Say their names...	60
Argyle Arcade, Glasgow	62
Charades with Kuya Resty	63
Screaming Blue...	64
I learned the truth	65
Requirement No. 13	66
How to clean a mirror	67
Red Cagoule	68
Whisht	69
Longley's Yard	70
The monkey in the car	71
On the morning bus...	72
The Swimmer	73
Saying Grace	74
The bust of Ferdinand Marcos at Tuba, Benguet.	75
Tinikling	77
Notes	78

Tatay Nick's

The small tear in my faded, ex-German
postal workers jacket that snagged on the nail
that held the string that held the lighter
at the door for single cigarette buyers
in Tatay Nick's sari-sari store
a week before our marriage.

I shovelled my palm into calamansi
like searching for the winning bingo ball,
two I stole to flavour the Ginebra
we might drink together that early morning.

His recipes passed on to grandchildren
massaged into their palms:
adobo, laing, ginataang libas
from leaves off the tree planted at the gate –
a seedling brought back from Bicol region
that now hues the loppy, tawny, dog
waiting to be walked.

On the living room rug he slept early,
curled into a question mark,
snoring through a western –
the stagecoach chased by arrows
on the flickering black and white screen
before the market run
in the dented Carter van.

Only his name above the store exists,
now they play mahjong on the green baize table,
clacking into the night, sipping shorts.
In the yard's swelter his dogs sniff and yelp.
I couldn't leave without mentioning the cats.
The one that followed us in a procession
up to the sepulchre, that clammy afternoon.
Marmalade smudged, ribs like a rack of knives,
it sat beside us whilst we prayed.

Another at the wedding-do as we toasted,
I felt a figure of eight
shift around my shins,
then at the last song it made itself seen.

Cosmonaut

Children dance and push
a council park roundabout
shaped like a flying saucer.
They spin it,
try to make it take off,
a child trapped in a cyclone
white-knuckled on a whirling
hulk of metal.
They throw their weight behind, thrust
and shove,
a thousand laughing mouths,
turning, turning,
until he's Gagarin
orbiting the Earth.

The blur slows to a stop,
to reveal a crew-cut boy
blinking
slashed in grease,
strewn with space dust.
He slides off into a pile,
seeing stars, he rises,
walks drunk,
plaiting legs,
falls.

I'm reminded of the babushka
with her offspring picking potatoes
carrying weight in an apron,
when a man falls from the sky
into the furrows of spuds.

Yuri dusted and shucked himself off
like a matryoshka doll.

The lad in the rec is upright,
he strolls forward,
leaving herringbone trainer prints,
his first baby steps on the moon.

Boy Nita's

The waiters are scraping Christmas stickers
off the window of the roadside café.
Adel is our friendly server today,
somewhere in her fifties, a missing tooth
which she tries to cover with her notepad.
In-between balancing plates of food
she damp-dusts figurines of the magi
removed from the *belén* with fairy-lights
and lined-up on the counter to be wrapped.
A table of thirteen are clinking glasses
while their teen punctuates the celebration
electrocuting mosquitos with swat racquet.
The TV reporter tells us:
that light rains are to dampen
The Black Nazarene procession.
A couple overheard near the *banyo*,
Children are part of society,
we could always adopt.
A scooter rider places his helmet
opposite on the table for two,
he drowns his *bangus* in *suka*.
We count out a tip for Adel and leave,
notice the empty space in the crib.

Coming to the fence

Witness the vixen caught on CCTV
framed in your doorbell cam screen.

There's a white goat on the garden wall
trimming the tops of the neighbour's privet.

A rangale of deer crossing Abbey Road,
one twerks its sporran of a tail at you.

Pull open the curtains wearing your rollers
to find piebald horses lounge on your lawn.

Sheep occupy McDonalds in Ebbw Vale,
'Flamingos are painting Mumbai pink'
and wild boar lick salty roads in Barcelona.

I'm back at the zoo in my father's arms
when the monkey stole my dummy and ran.

Peeling pomelo

The first slit into open pores
like an early surgeon
mapping out veins, locating the heart.
I am tasked with peeling for the dessert,
warned not to pierce the pink flesh,
and release the juice.
I try silently running my fingers
under the skin of the fruit,
the sound of someone sucking their teeth.

Here, my naive knife work, displayed
rotating on the Lazy Susan.
The segments glisten like stuck-out tongues
on a family photograph.
At dinner, conversations take tangents
before asking the parents' permission.

Wake

We take a cab to the Chapel of Rest,
dicing traffic in Metro Manila,
rain on glass makes mincemeat out of us.
We press coins into flesh of our cabbie –
his leather palms sweaty.
The taxi like a confessional box,
mossy stepping-stones to avoid this mud.

The only dead body I'd seen in the flesh
was my grandad – Rab.
I caught his waxed reflection
in the foxed dressing table mirror –
before stepping into the bedroom.
The tortoiseshell comb –
the one he wrapped paper around and blew
his tune – a cowboy by the campfire.

This man I never knew.
In the visitor's book I knot
my initials like newly laced shoes.
He's drawn a crowd from as far as Sheffield.
You pull me in by the fingertips,
he's encased in a dome of glass as if for sale.
His nails are like polished almonds –
the lunala rising from finger-bed.
The eyes, convex like upturned teaspoons
left on the Formica tabletop.
Lips pursed, the last conversation they had.

'Equalizer'

Arms clasped at the dip of his lumber spine,
smooth against the silk sheen of his waistcoat –
bowler hat tipped.
He watches two sons ride one enamelled steed
of the galloper carousel.

The horse's feet never touch the ground,
steamed-up, they go around like a zoetrope –
under the mushroom spokes of the awning.
The father's shadow laid out in front
like a drunk man in the Hall of Mirrors.

One of these boys, forty odd years on,
will flutter a betting slip that breaks him,
watching his jockey-less nag cross the line,
that keeps running until lathered.

The Tubig Man

You'll hear him
mid-afternoon
on his round.

Bowed knees
pedal the bones
of a tricycle

under the umbrella
with tassels.
Imagine the colour.

The glug
of water
delivered to door,

slumped in plastic
like lifting
a fat baby.

He shouts,
'Tubig, Tubig!'
with his father's voice.

Daredevil

Evel Knievel wound up to the hilt,
about to unzip the road from number 14.
Last outing, left unconscious in my room,
his leg twisted, head back-to-front,
hip ball and socket popped.

We had shifted on from piddling toys.
A first frost grows across the top lip,
and pimples are a missed dartboard wall,
Woody looking startled from pellet shot.

We string the rope for a hanging,
thread the stick like a pocket watch chain
and pull straws for the running order -
I came out last.

There are five of us today on the bank,
taking turns to Tarzan out into the road
as if launching a new ship,
it's summer Sunday evening, our necks browned.

The lorry driver pumps his foot hard
like putting something out of its misery.
Flesh and bones sing.
Our mucker set out laughing before the hit
as if flying to the moon.

My mother is scrubbing the doorstep clean,
Where've you been? You're black as the ace of spades.

Yellow Brick Road

We are choosing a pair of shoes together,
Maaari ba kitang tulungan sir/ ma'am?
We prefer to do this together.
I select the simple red slippers,
like the feel of a rose bloom as a kid
you are told off for touching.
I also bring a selection of granny shoes
just for your reaction.
I assist after finding your size,
get you to sit, you offer your foot.
Perfect and affordable.
You stand, take a walk, stare
for a while in the angled mirror.
At the wedding do, I notice you slightly
hitch-up your dress on the path for photos
then click your heels together three times.

Majorettes

It's the summer Springsteen is on fire,
they practice for hours on end in the park
for the Miner's gala,
twirling wands into an X,
like plane propellers.
The sound of nipsy players
whacking hickory sticks,
pommelling ovoid pottys into space.

A man carries a Christmas bag in May,
clicking his tongue at the Jack Russell.
We stop off to natter to Mr. Bell
at the entrance of the nursing home,
to test him about football clubs and grounds.
Liver spots pattern his hands
Roy and Dave pass by from coal picking,
pushing their donkey-bike laden with loot.

On their day,
Carol is angelic on glockenspiel,
against a palette of South Yorkshire grey.
Alison is run over with a lint roller.
She will march
behind a hoisted, red, colliery banner.
They will play 'Dancing in the Dark' on brass.
Ali flings her baton into the air,
her open palms still waiting for the catch.

The men who sleep in trucks

park up in line at service stations
the way his boys lined up toy Corgis
on the front room carpet at Christmas.
In the rear view, one trucker checks his hair,
gut dropping out of a red polo shirt.
Tasselled curtains drawn and pegged
just like his mother thirty years back.
Hear the music bleeding from cabs,
this one's window wound down – a last smoke.
Their lot is leaving the wife –
a Penelope finding her own rhythms.
You'll hear them on late night radio phone-ins,
their loose change dropped in a fisherman's sock
for toll charges.
Bring into focus Bob, tapping out a text,
Townes Van Zandt, full blast:
Being born is going blind
And buying down a thousand times.
Then sometimes, girls in silver hot pants,
he waits for the knuckle-tapped coded knock.

The Scaffolders' Daytime Disco

Pete sings the wrong words
with the Bee Gees harmonies,
Bald headed woman
More than a woman to me.
His repartee for eight years.

Then there's the banter –
the ribbing of the teenager
flaunting his tattooed
black panther swishing its tail
on the swell of his bicep.

Their choice of station
booms over the garden wall
unsettling the man's false teeth
over a late French breakfast.
The Times wrung out like laundry.

Hydraulic tools blast,
after the elevenses,
keep you on your toes.
Two spanners paradiddle
like prison code tapped on pipes.

A silly, loud scream
from the top tier of planks.
A bare-chested man
thinks he's Tarzan of the Apes,
doing semaphore with wasps.

All is quiet now,
boots poke out of van windows.
There's concentration
eating homemade sandwiches
like snogging in an alley.

The apprentice texts,
sat alone on a warm wall,
kicking his riggers.
He sends his most tender words,
like unwinding a crabbing line.

A painter on rungs
tries to cut in a straight edge –
tongue's a turtle's head.
He ponders being fifty,
I know I need a small vacation...

Mangos

We stand on the *kanto*
waiting for a tricycle.

The mangos are ready to drop,
for the villagers to pick-up.

We were just unmarried then,
clasping hands within the week.

Scent of fruit ripening
amongst clothes,
unpacking my suitcase.

Pagmamaneho sa timog

I pull from my wardrobe your dad's barong,
hang it – shoulders and all – from the door casing,
billowing and twisting in the wind,
the sleeves reach out a hand.
Then I tugged at my cuff in company
of godparents to keep tattoos concealed.
A long drive to the party in Batangas
like the Beverly Hillbillies,
teaching me to count and days of the week:
isa, dalawa, tatlo...

Cooks having a crafty smoke at the stove,
turning Cebu lechon over a pit of coals
and the pig is smiling at his fate,
basted in his toffee-coloured glaze.
There's a private chapel strung in lights,
a life-size plastic Jollibee looks on.
The men in the group drink two fingers
of Emperador brandy – they call *Empi*
and point with their lips at the bottle
to hand it around the circle.
You're laid on your back like Huck Finn
only a big toe twitching
like a stub of ginger.

We are sat at the table waiting for food,
you mention your fondness for Glen Campbell
'I hear you singin' in the wire.'
I'm chewing on a something going nowhere.
We are planning to become family
and it's more photos stored on a phone
to be shared online with OFWs.
In Sheffield, I am pulling creases
from your barong I may wear tomorrow –
a tang of smoke wafts, catches my throat.

How to bring down a chimney stack

Climb high.
Fred Dibnah's silhouette up a chimney,
after a pint or two.
This dirty faced, Milk Tray man
ascends a cigar of a tower.
He gawks into the camera, too close,
like he sees you sprawled out on the sofa.

His unfashionable jumpers
are white noise on T.V.
His flat-cap, the colour of Swarfega
made so from rubbing greasy palms.
*This contraption came from watching
steeplejacks from the 40's and 50's.*

The milk churn shoots up, a flying Dalek,
Fred flees over tussocky fields.
Arms folded he stands back and watches,
as fag ash droops in pursed lips.

The rubber-pumped horn at ground zero,
policemen circle with arms cuffed behind backs
keeping local spectators at a distance.
A lad on his Chopper, snorkel hood up,
sucks an ice-lolly.
Run!
Fred looks into the screen,
smudges soot across his cheek, another notch.

Kevin

In Marikina, a lola clings to the roof,
like a maya bird in the morning sun,
on screens for everybody to see
after the ire of Typhoon Ulysses.
Coyote brown flood water rising
as if earth plates are moving.
A large wooden boot for the old woman,
'so many children, she didn't know what to do.'
it's peeled from a shop sign taken down-river.
A pet owner is reunited
with his dog called Kevin.

Gym-rat

My teenage son bulks up on Creatine
3.5 scoops = three chicken breasts.
He squats as if the globe is on his back,
becomes light-headed, suffers nosebleeds,
then chins up to the bar
like hanging from a cliff edge.
A tee shirt peeled off like Cellophane,
pumped after pulling at the pec-deck.

Watching him pose in the foxed mirror,
spreading his lats like a threatened cobra,
mouthing his mantra, *check out the guns,*
squeezing a bicep into a tennis ball.
I open the door, feel his skin blushing,
the tuppence birthmark on his back defaced.

Mulligan Stew

The Rubby-Dubs are passing round the hooch,
Come in my friend, come in, join the circle.
One wipes the lip of the green bottle
with his shirt tail,
hands me a *swally of Jesus' blood* –
wears a reddened glow from the brazier.

They've strung up some device to hang a pot,
big as a call to prayer cathedral bell.
Hangin' from an 'S' hook Mulligan stew
bubbles like blinking chameleon eyeballs.

Traffic drones along the overhead bridge,
fathers taking kids back to ex-wives,
a bus driver clackin' gum in the rear view.

Apart from Maisie-Ann, we are all men,
but others wouldn't call us that.
Punch-drunk Jeb mics a wooden spoon -
*I like the green grass under my shoes,
what can I lose? I'm flat, that's that.*

We flip beer crates, take a pew.
My big toes swollen like radishes,
the veins in my feet mapped like rivers –
the stench of it all.

Silodrome

This young man's skull rattling in his helmet
like two dice shaken in a cup,
the sound of a marble on a roulette wheel,
rubberneckers peer down into the well.
Under the ticket collector's counter
his first ever customer's coin,
held by crossed nails for luck
like lovers striking their mark
into the bark of a secret woodland oak.
This shilling rubbed each business morning,
smoothing down the crown,
he hopes to pass on to his eldest.
That's if he'll marry and all that follows.
His son's a Jack without a Jill,
there's been many, but they do not stay.
His boy's the centre of this compass,
where it stops, nobody knows...

Miriam

walks into the sea fully clothed,
her pockets bobbing,
the sand underfoot sucks.

She keeps on, as always,
sliced by waves, a magician's girl
waggling a toe for the audience.

At the waist, she feels the tug of her child,
then up to the breasts, the suckling pull
on her nipple.

Now she's pinned against a wall,
her husband's thumb prints like petals
strung round her neck.

Her toes pointed like a ballerina,
dibbed into the softness,
she rises floating on water.

The Shed

We work from the bottom up,
replacing the rotten slats
that crumble between the fingers,
the good bits are a woodworm dartboard.

At 77, my father on his knees,
crouched tight like working in the mines
knocking in props.

Only now, he's trying to hammer in nails
to the panels, with his essential tremors.
Greedy-boards line the skip for junk
which I fish out, set aside.
We stop-up fallen windows
with thumb printed putty.

After the painting has gone off
I wash the mossy panes from the outside,
he washes from the inside – waving,
and in this light, he looks peely-wally.

Drawing a diagram for my mother, for the courts, for a deaf compensation claim

I draw around a miniature whiskey
bottle to mark out her workstation.
We are looking from an overview.
There's an entrance but no doors.
She faces a four-foot wall, looking over
to the trimming tables,
etching rubber offcuts.
Beyond that are the men's pressers
moulding hot-water bottles
that come out like gutted piglets.
She mentions her shift pattern, 2 'til 10,
feeding her life onto a card into a clock.
This is my third attempt,
because she's 'going back forty odd years'.
We waited up in pyjamas,
'til she came back smiling with a late night snack.
She recalls wolf-whistles,
but sticks up her wedding ring finger,
mouthing something they'd have to lip-read,
like gossiping women over the garden fence –
rollers parcelled in headscarves.
I finish the plan and she stands,
dusts down her skirt, flicks the kettle.
I ask, 'did you like the job?'
She doesn't hear, opens the fridge for supper.

French Lesson

'Over on the other side of the fence'
the medium says, between sips of tea.
Far from giving release, she makes us tense,

sat around her table for the séance.
She calls up Arthur, heart attack at sea,
over on the other side of the fence.

Press play and record as she commences,
watch eye-lids twitch, raspy she speaks out *'oui.'*
Far from giving release she makes us tense.

We tell her, 'Arthur couldn't speak no French.'
Open eyed now she looked straight through me,
over to the other side of the fence.

He'd learnt off the other woman. *'Il pense*,
he thinks you would have liked her, his *Aimée.'*
Far from giving release she makes us tense.

'Before grandma', she whispers his defence.
'The mortal pain is lifted, he's now free'.
Over on the other side of the fence,
far from giving release she leaves us tense.

One at a time...

In the church hall, we are in a circle.
Tony offloads, Vicky wants it all back.
She tells of being holed-up in her parent's.
He strives to rub tattoos off his knuckles
while recalling working at Butlin's,
trying to explain to a girl,
stopping at one is impossible,
and how he must climb through each day.

At the speaker meetings, I clench fists,
vowing that tomorrow will be different.
When I leave with Jim, he keeps talking
about the twelve steps and twenty odd years
and how these days he spots morning buds
opening on branches.

The following afternoons I chuck empties
into the bottle bank like loading
a submarine with missiles.

Sirens

I am staggering up West Bar
plaiting my legs, then stop
at the Fire and Police Museum.
Looking through the glass doors
at the parked engines.

I realise I'd been here before –
eight years old, on a school trip.
I was picked out of the crowd to climb
to the Simon engine's passenger seat
where firefighters gripped the leather seat
or back to the station like a miner
sweaty, sooty and tear-streaked.
They let me sound the siren.

Thirty-two years on,
I jump out of my skin,
staring at myself in the window,
drunk and my ears still ringing.

Northern Soul

They claimed he was panivorous,
I look it up on my shielded phone.
I wonder what he'd make of his spread
should he be at his wake.
He's encased in a glass dome,
like a 1950's Buick convertible
or a glass dome keeping the flies off a pie,
and other indigestibles.
I wonder if they will make him a pack-up
or a piece to break the journey.
I'm tickled with that laughter
like the kids in *Kes* being lectured
in the headmaster's office
about to get the cane.
I am sweating, clenching my fists
into my thighs that feel like dough –
I know.
I'm sure there is a light dusting of flour
on the floor.
And then Dobie Gray fades in –
'Out on the floor each night, I'm really moving'.

The Robin

He's telling the one about the robin *again*.
Daily he sat and held bread upon his hand,
or a translucent strip of bacon rind,
feet splayed like wire on his palm.

They're away on holiday
the bird was trapped in the garage,
tapping dusty glass at dawn
leaving beak marks like pellet shot.
When found, its head limp as cloth.
Eyes sealed like a slot screwdriver.

He's started losing other things:
spectacles, mother's crucifix, comb,
and turns on his step halfway down the drive,
as if looking for a trail of breadcrumbs.

The Ticklish Butcher

His blue and white pinstripe trousers yanked down,
in the cellar toilet, he's feeling his way
inside her white dress he knows
as well as cuts of the cow on the wall map,
and they always have a smile for the patrons.

Almost lunchtime, he's pressed up at the till,
cashing in, watching the clock
when she sidles in – tickles him.

Rabbits strung from their back feet,
devoid of speed,
like a lady's open wardrobe door.

After dinner break, she rises
in her whites, to sweep the shop floor,
a tendril falls from her net hat,
she tucks it back into place
then strews sawdust, like scattering seed
and they always have a smile for the patrons.

Club trip

That's the corner where we once clustered,
our annual club trip to the coast.
Children circled like a merry-go-round,
my brother's hair parted down,
freckled cheeks like spattered marmalade.
They handed out green pound notes in envelopes
as 'spendo' for fairground rides and flashing lights.

Where children tip-toed against height markers,
while old folks flick plastic eyelids shut
playing *bingo!*
On the beach echoes of 50's 'rock 'n' roll,
candyfloss beards, ice-cream rainbow dusted.
A parent towel dried her child's feet,
buffing toenails as if smoothing pebbles.

The miners always looked out of place here,
their twenty deck of John Player Specials
turned up in tee-shirt sleeves.
It was the tattooed coal dust eyeliner
that marked them out.
Today their children's eyes are shadowed.

The Rowan Tree

Zooming in using a satellite map
the patchwork fields,
then closer roads unravelling
parachuting to my childhood garden.
Gone is the rowan tree to tangle me,
only a bruised mark on the lawn.

Where my world was turned upside-down,
tiger striped hiding amongst leaves
up high, my carved, KR, 1984.
The blossom froth fell like confetti,
the trusses of scarlet polished berries
pentagram marked to offer protection,
according to some old wives,
and things I saw, were left in the branches.

Music Row

I have known drunks who would play chicken,
bare-chested and slashed like a punk
pogoing out of a crowd.
This one put his fists through a windowpane
and snatched the new VHS
from a terraced lounge recording a soap,
then walked up the road like a horror film.

The man never seen from number 14,
milk bottles left with notes on the doorstep,
the perfume of bath suds in summer
spurts from the sock of the drainpipe
on Saturday nights.

That man steps into the street, faces him down.
His door wide open for all to see.
Johnny Cash sings, *My Grandfather's Clock,*
the vinyl scratched and ticking away...

Tommy Murray's brolly

Tommy Murray's brolly, the last thing I have.
The way he did the Charlie Chaplin twirl
down the road, into the sunset.
Whiff of Woodbine smoke clings to the inside
when raised this Tuesday morning.
Leather smoothed handle like his bald head
patterned with liver spots.
I'm holding his hand at that pelican-crossing
on our way to the library for Westerns.
While I am cross-legged on the parquet
listening to the Librarian reading,
The Hungry Caterpillar
eating through anything in its way,
I see him frowning, chewing things over,
rolling his sorrows with his tobacco
and I know he'll wince tell me,
It'll be alright.
I ram the umbrella into a litter bin
like a broken crow
and hope the rain will cleanse me.

Joey

My aunt discovered condensed milk
could stick hearth tiles better than Superglu.
The year men would take a van
to go lamping rabbits with lurchers
and a borrowed garden fork
to wrestle turnips by moonlight.

Our shoes came from a donation box
paired up and tied at the soup kitchen,
and Fred Taylor staggered home in two odd shoes.

They played pool at the club on afternoons,
their gold signet rings have been pawned
only the hue of nicotine on fingers
as they line up for a shot.
They look strange in this sun
without the rims of their eyes tattooed
like a woman on the morning doorstep.

I remember most the green budgie
They had taught to speak the words:
scab, scab, scab.
The blue one wouldn't say a thing.

The Mirror Man

As we pull to a stop at the junction
there he is again sitting on the bench,
talking to himself in his vanity glass.
He's like a bloody budgie.
Workmates laugh, bang the van.
I'm shuffling in my seat.

He's held together with string,
newspapers wrapped around his shins,
hair the colour of dripping.
A wrist flick, he flashes this morning light,
playing ping-pong with the sun.

The green signal moves us on
to the site where we sign-in,
ten minutes late for the foreman.

At breakfast in the café, I pick out
The Mirror Man, 2.15 at Haydock
which romps home.
I hope the same for him.

Malaya Never Again

tattooed on his bicep,
flexed into a cooking apple.
Text arcs the soldier in a jungle hat,
the size of a plastic toy,
shooting from the hip.
The arm is stretched taut
as rubber on a drawn catapult.
The man bends his knees,
allows his grandchild hook on
and lifts him to the sky,
dangling from arm branches.
Small feet get purchase,
walk up the grandfather's trunk,
until he's crossing ropes,
on an assault course.
The boy drops his legs,
makes it to the neck into a cuddle,
but stamped on this ex-squaddie's mind,
those years he's been trying to block out.

The Snog

after Pete McKee

These two are not new to this game,
bigger than life, watched by the city.
If you stayed in the same place,
you'd feel the sun warm your cheeks
then fade and peel away,
not to mention rain doing paradidles.
You'd hope she'd have a Rainmate
to complement his tweed flat cap.

He slips cold hands inside her coat,
like a teenager at the bus stop.
What's happening in there?
She reaches for the clouds of his shoulders,
clung like a koala.

You want to place them in an age
of pigeon lofts, a raffle of betting slips,
and the bingo caller ringing in her ears.
His Velcro 'chin-pie' stubble will not grow,
her cheeks will always keep blushing.

Jubilee

I can't tell you what *it* was at infants,
forced them to screw me to a stool,
in a corner facing the main road.
I could hear myself breathing,
then traffic fades in, gears changing –
the deliveries of labelled bloods,
a convoy of travellers in caravans.
There was something to do with the Queen,
when they handed out mintage in pouches.
My father was out of work,
mother half deaf making tennis balls,
notching up the nights.
The need to be outside of things.
It's lodged inside like a coin in a call box.
If I could unjam it, speak to myself
in my eighth year and hammer it out.
Why are bare legs still plastered to that seat?
Why does *it* keep coming back?

Musculoskeletal Imaging

Most have one if you tense,
a snuff box joint.
Radiography class, year 1.
That quicksilver light that sees inside,
I recall my own x-ray,
a fracture of the fifth metacarpal.
Wallace's Monument, denim flares,
my arm head-locked around my brother's neck
tussling behind an unaware mother
posing for holiday snaps
long before their divorce.
What could I have done these following years?
We fight on, it plays over like a Chinese burn.

Afore ye go

Let's crack the collar of that last bottle –
a deoch-an-doras.
At the hearth, silverfish scuttle,
your laugh the sound of a mule.

You tell the one about Sandy Bells,
that guy who tried to sell you the thumb
of an Egyptian dentist called Ramses –
but that was a proper digit in that box.
You know, my folks were drunk when they made me,
I never sobered up.

We move on from Jesus,
drift onto the time you smuggled a mannequin
upstairs at the back of the bus
while the driver was smoking
and left her to go for a joyride.

The 'Take a Break' roadside trailer shutters
are down – about to open.
The chef unshaven, gleams in whites,
haloed by the winter sun, winding his watch.
We drink coffee in polystyrene cups.
On the common, a dog chews a dildo,
and we've no phonecam charge between us
as proof.

Hail Mary

And while his father was in the newsagents
buying tobacco, chatting up the cashier,
he reached for the family claw hammer,
and smashed the dials of the van,
going at the mileage they'd done,
the speed at which they'd taken to get here.
Things would not be the same from this point.
There had been other signs:
rashers pegged out on the washing line,
the mystery of the garrotted dog.

The rosary hanging from the rear-view mirror
is unhooked, and each bead is threaded
through finger and thumb.
He sees his dad exit the shop, smile,
unwrap a Hamlet from the cream pack,
click and spin the Zippo on his thigh, exhale,
like the cigar on hearing the birth of his son.

Too daft to laugh at

my father would say at Tommy Cooper,
yet twinkled his toe, popping through work socks,
white as a golf-ball lost in undergrowth,
come back Peter, come back Paul.

He'd snooze in the corner with his crossword,
pocket dictionary opened on his chest,
I imagined the light shade upon his head
like a cock-eyed fez.

Sunday afternoon after carving the joint,
nearly a gallon of booze
fermenting in his gut.
He popped the buttons on my best shirt,
like scattering a bowl of tiddlywinks.
Fists pinned me up against the dresser,
knocking over ornaments
the balanced head of the shepherd fell.

He sidled away into the other room,
belt un-buckled,
I'm left thinking he'd nearly lamped me,
just like that.

Lolo in Levi's

Finding a way into this poem,
tricky as packing a *balikbayan* box
sent back from OFWs.
You see them on the conveyor belt
the globe squeezed into a square
from diasporic addresses
of the Filipino spread
their *kababayans* forced to cross oceans,
to provide for their families.

Ate Jen working the NHS frontline,
Kuya Don in the Middle East,
or Erika cleaning in Barcelona.
All watch siblings grow via a phone screen,
or bedtime stories in the afternoon.

Boxes are filled with candy,
letters, books, and tins of Spam.
Cast off clothing with life still in them,
or basketball vests and baseball hats.

On my return to Metro Manila
I am weighing scales with *pasalubong*.
We will have a home welcoming meal
with cousins hardly recognisable.

Firstly, I pick out my old Dickies shirt,
a cousin in my pair of combat boots,
my checked shirt on my aunt –
it's my personal *ukay-ukay* store.

Then my Levi's 501s on my lolo
that knock ten years off him,
the amount of time we have lost.

Waiting for Arthur

At Ye Olde Murenger House, Newport
I order two pints of Abbot ale,
you claimed was made with holy water,
and a pair of double whiskey chasers.
I leave two glasses at the end of the bar,
tell the landlord I'm saving it for someone,
and take our seat in the corner.

What he would re-tell today?
There's the one about going AWOL
after the war,
how he wouldn't take the drilling,
instead selling stolen clothes
on the black-market in Liverpool.
I imagine him in my cast-off Levi cords,
the scuffed work boots that keep him upright.

Then the time between arguments
between Trots and Tankies in Canada,
then hitching it down to America,
or jumping ship in Australia
having a swally with the 'rubby-dubs'
sipping liniment around a brazier.

We could laugh at the firefighter's demo,
missing the coach back to Wales,
jumped the train,
helped by a supportive RMT guard.

The last time I saw Arth
was a parting glass at the rugby club,
I heard the crowds roar from the stands,
while I stood at the urinal.

As the brass ship bell rings last orders,
two glasses stand on the end of the bar,
untouched.

Say their names...

Balita.
Metro Manila Ngayon.
27-year-old Vincent Adia is shot and left to bleed with a carton that says 'pusher.'

The headlines play on a bar room TV,
and drinkers pay little attention,
but the barman aims the remote
and turns on the subtitles.

It is 4am on the boundary,
Vincent takes three slugs to the head
on the streets of Barangay San Isidro.
His killers use a black pentel pen
to inscribe a message now unreadable
'awash in the dark red of Vincent's blood.'

Medics find three entry wounds
that formed a triangle on his left cheek.
One exited behind his right ear,
another went through his right jaw.

Vincent communicates through sign language.
He hand-signs his first name,
for his last name, he points
 to a tattoo on his wrist that said 'Adia.'

He wears a suit of tattoos,
names like graffiti tags
cover his upper body,
but looking on in sorrow
the Virgin Mary on his chest.

At 11am hospital employees
keep an eye on the clock,
hold their rumbling guts,
about to begin their lunch.

The masked gunman steps into the hospital,
walks straight to the front of Vincent's bed,
shoots him once then turns the gun on staff
to kiss the ground
then twice, he finishes the job.

After hours of walkie-talkie static
outside the emergency room.
Where were the police?
Chief Corpuz says it was a case
of (bad coincidence).

They try to jigsaw the victim's past
sketch out a picture of his character
from ex-partners and friends.

Days before, he visited his mother
to borrow P50 for a haircut,
his birthday looming on Halloween.
Black locks drop,
swept up, placed in a bin with the rest.
Who would think to take a keepsake curl
for his mother to wear around her neck?

Kuya! Bartender! Can we order?
The TV shows a speech by Duterte,
he points the remote at the President,
and flicks the channel to the basketball.

Argyle Arcade, Glasgow

Early evening darkness is drawing in,
groups of shoppers puff out cold fog.
Lured by the L-shaped Victorian arcade,
more than thirty diamond merchants,
it's like *Christmas every day* in here –
this site of former tenement lodgings.
I think I hear ghosts of domestic echoes
mingling amid seasonal chatter.

The polished nails of a shop assistant,
clutch for jewels behind glass,
like a fun-fair candy-grabber.
A young couple gaze and point at rings,
his thumb hooks her stretch-denim back pocket
the girl's palm is suckered to the window.
Between them they calculate payment plans
and it hurts my eyes to look.

Charades with Kuya Resty

I point to the floor,
he's no idea.
I unlace my boot.
Mga bota?
I yank at my sock,
hop and point.
Paa?
I make my fingers like scissors,
Ah, mga paa – feet!

What is itchy?
I scratch my body
like a chimpanzee
picking off fleas.
Hindi ko naiintindihan.
Nosebleed!
I walk my fingers across the table,
stretch out arms and hum.
A tinfoil holder as telescope,
I squint to look overseas,
but in the end, I must get up and leave.

Screaming Blue

It's whistle-blown now,
the outer shell of the building
charred on the skyline.

'The fire floors we went in
were helmet meltingly hot.'

They, that had travelled to this island,
housed and clad in,
those that huddled together
in one room after Ramadan –
the numbers they will keep schtum.

'When I got down and removed my tunic
my shoulders were burnt.'

Stairwells smoke logged
from cyanide cladding,
shapes formed in the mind,
trying to push forward through dark
like deep sea diving.

And now I look at Grenfell,
after the ruckus.
It stands like a game of Jenga.

I learned the truth

To those miners glad to come home,
to sit at the dinner table,
freshly showered and smelling of lemons.
Knife and fork held in both hands,
you couldn't miss the coal eyeliner.
Dexys are topping the charts in dungarees,
siblings and friends pull faces, raise eyebrows.
A kick under the table,
you'd think we were at a séance.

Shift forward,
      my father no longer has panda eyes,
he carries a gold ingot room to room,
the twenty 'bennies' and his Zippo.
At all hours he haunts the house.

I stare at myself in my own mirror,
the lines on my face are my father's
and I catch that look –
the one saying,
      'all lives are not considered equal.'

The BBC reports rocket attacks
from Palestine
switching the chronology of events
as they did in Orgreave,
strikers turned up in t-shirts and trainers.

I hear my father's finger end
stabbing the dinner table
as if diffing out the sixth cigarette
into the chipped glass ashtray.
A coronet of cigarette smoke
rises slow as a seahorse.

Requirement No. 13

The above named are to be assessed
by the U.K. Decision Making Centre.
Please provide the following documents:
your wedding and family photographs.

Will they look into our eyes,
or at a certain way of holding hands
to point out something not ringing true?
And then the transcripts of conversations,
will they twist and frame what was spoken?

But what about what was not said?
We decide not to mention the priest
who wore trainers underneath his vestments,
only photographed from the waist up.

How to clean a mirror

I'd usually scrunch headlines without thought,
the way my mother showed us with clenched fist,
to leave streak free mirrors so the wealthy
might smile at their full sets of teeth,
before dressing for dinner in barong.
A selection of shoes stood in line,
and I'd step from pair to pair when alone,
as if crossing a river on wet stones.

I scour away smears and traces of perfume,
the lines of my brow furrow like *inay*'s
something of her eyes looking through me.

'It's all over, Marcos flees!'
A picture of the wimpled sister
facing up on EDSA
to a soldier wearing a bullet belt
like the smile of a skull.
Her glasses smudged with fingerprints.

Today, in a hotel room
I work as one of the many *invisibles*.
'*Bong Bong*' Marcos shouting on mute TV.
I wipe the static from that man's mouth.

Red Cagoule

A tambourine shake of coins in my pockets
that he'll clutch and dig into his palms
just before the final whistle.
I will keep his sweated head protected,
a map of liver spots on his bald napper.
When he draws my cords to a pucker
I make him a gnome fishing for a catch.

It's the scent of my lining in the warm car
after we have lost.
My secret pouch holds Mint Imperials
for the journey home,
listening to scores on the radio.
The chafe on his nape – my love bite.

Whisht

You strike a blue-capped safety match
in our dark dorm room.
The sulphurous flame makes you old,
as if about to enter, stage left
in the make-up of the villain,
teeth stained by tannins of cheap Malbec.
It burns down to the cuticle.

We'd snuck up to the gate on a tricycle,
the full moon of headlight, tick of engine,
as we whispered and counted out coins
into the calloused palm of our driver –
a rosary swayed in the neon lit cab,
Salamat Po – Shush.

My birthday has just tipped up and over
into autumn.
There's a feeling the Welsh call *hiraeth*.
I toss five pesos,
slap to back of hand and ponder.
The tang of currency on my fingers,
Aguinaldo's bust gazing into space,
what's left, is a kind of silence.
Eastwards over the sea someone sings.

Longley's Yard

Iron bergs – we think – are punchouts
from sheets of metal
left in piles like a coal delivery.
We fill our pockets,
make our eyes into a spirit level.
We wrap a patch of leather
around the missile, draw back the elastic
of the catapult.

Some take aim at the magpie
bobbing in its dinner suit
but I let rip at school windows,
it pelts straight through the math's class.

And whenever I hear *Spiegel im Spiegel*
it fetches those times back,
cutting a hole in a fence
to load with ammo.

The monkey in the car

parked up in the supermarket,
like the one that stole my dummy
in a Scottish zoo
that my dad managed to grab back.

But he's gone now and here I am,
staring at a monkey in a car,
its tiny Action Man hands
grip the steering wheel.

Sporting a red jacket with gold trim,
like theatre curtains parting.
I notice he has cast his hat,
upturned like a strewn medicine cup.

As I depart, my reflection
in the driver's window –
my father's face, how he held his head.

On the morning bus

I am sat behind a Filipino mom.
I now grasp a peppering of words in Tagalog.
She holds up her phone to eye-level,
I see a child eating dinner at a table,
seven hours ahead of us driving through drizzle.
Kain tayo, the infant calls out, offers
a morsel on a fork,
then flies it into her buttonhole mouth.
The mommy's image in the top right corner
of the screen is wearing a facemask,
it's loops her ears in a figure of eight.
Often these OFWs commute
to work up to their elbows
on sickbay wards, tending other's children.
This kid, so happy to see her *inay*.
Then, with a flick of the wrist
I'm a stranger on a bus at their *salu-salo*.

The Swimmer

The first toe like a nub of ginger
breaks through the surface.
This is Colombo, 2022.
It might be a fine year to pop corks.

So, go swim in the President's pool,
thrust through the chlorinated stench,
become the fish noticed by a worker
on the riverbank during a strike.

After a lap, pop-up like a seal,
the people muster around the edge.
You are interviewed on the BBC,
you tell them, 'I am so happy',
and not just any old happiness.

The palace is a tourist attraction,
folk feel the ply of the red carpet,
where a lone cleaner would flick the wire
dreaming of being like a ringmaster.

Another length, hold your breath,
emerge into a new society.
Make Ned Merrill and cross boundaries.

Saying Grace

Your aunt is the one to clear her throat.
We bow heads as the prayer is spoken.
The eye of the *bangus* stares,
I feel the revolving breeze of the fan
shift the hairs on my suede nape.

There is much I want to ask
as we spin servings on the Lazy Susan.
I want us to sit at the table,
as 'man and wife' and clink glasses.

Immigration rules hinder what will be.
There may not be a break in the fence,
I doubt there will be any children.

Just because you were born
in the muggy heat of Manila,
I, across open pages of an atlas,
where my T-shirt tanned arms are now fading.

Your mother still sets out a place
for your father two years gone.

Bust of Ferdinand Marcos at Tuba, Benguet

A taxi driver from across the way
agreed a price to take us on a tour.
His notched face and loosened tongue,
told us about –
'a vast and thoughtless head of concrete
looked down from shrubs over the land,
the *wrinkled lip, and sneer of cold command.*
Thirty metres high they built his greased quiff,
two years 'til completion, the year of 1980.
It's claimed the Ibaloi were forced to sell
their land for low, low prices.
They drained blood from pig and carabao
and flooded the bust in an exorcism.
This followed the '86 People's Revolution
where placards read:
Suko Na!
Talo Ka Na!
Marcos Layas Na!
In short, You've lost! Marcos run away!
Then just after Christmas in 2002
treasure hunters or New People's Army
did what you see today.'

Did the dynamite make Marcos sing?
Were they like The Numskulls
whispering into the President's ear?
His brains are now blown inside out,
they've left him barely a frown.

You'll have heard his words aired by satellite,
under the shadow of Imelda,
her sculptured hair, heels perched in stilettos.
Look on my Works, ye Mighty, and despair!

Our tour guide fans himself,
with a waft of banknotes
slotted between his fingers and thumb,
he sneezes three times.

A long toot at the horn as we sound off
into a wheelspin leaving enough
dust to pack the nostrils like snuff.

Tinikling

It was when you leaned over and whispered,
after our meal, the stick dance started,
and you taught me the word *tinikling*.

I could feel the tamp, tamp of bamboo poles
rise from floor to white flab of my thighs
and you'd never seen a dancer snapped
like a rabbit in a gin-trap.

We were on a two-for-one deal,
I wondered if I should sell my watch,
strapped to the inside of my wrist – ticking.

Your legs stiff as chopsticks,
under the table cross around mine
which is when I knew.

We sit upright,
two chess pieces – king and queen.

Notes

Tatay Nick's
Tatay is Tagalog for 'Father'. A *sari-sari* is a small shop based in the community that sells everyday general items. *Calamansi* is a citrus hybrid predominantly cultivated in the Philippines. Ginebra is a brand of gin made by Ginebra, San Miguel Inc.

Boy Nita's
Belén is the Spanish name for Bethlehem, the birthplace of Jesus. It was an unusual word I came across in the Philippines for the nativity scene. *Banyo* means 'bathroom' in Tagalog, *bangus* 'milkfish' and *suka* 'vinegar'.

The Tubig Man
Tubig is 'water' in Tagalog.

Yellow Brick Road
Maaari ba akong tulungan ka sir / ma'am? means 'Can I help you sir / ma'am?'

Mangos
Kanto means 'corner'.

Pagmamaneho sa timog
translates as 'driving south'. A *barong* is an embroidered formal shirt for men and the national dress of the Philippines. OFWs are Overseas Filipino Workers; the term is often used to refer to Filipino migrant workers, people with Filipino citizenship who reside in another country for a limited period of employment. *Lechon* is roasted pig. *Jollibee* is a Filipino multinational chain of fast-food restaurants.

Kevin
Lola means 'grandmother'.

Lolo in Levi's

Lolo means 'grandfather'. *Balikbayan*, loosely translated, means 'to return home'. A *kababayan* is a 'compatriot'. *Ate* means 'older sister'. *Kuya* means 'brother'; the word is also used as an address to an older man. *Pasalubong* is the Filipino tradition of travellers bringing gifts to people back home. An *ukay-ukay* is a Philippine store where second-hand items such as clothes, bags, shoes and other accessories are sold at a cheap price. Items sold at the *ukay-ukay* are commonly imported from North American or European countries.

Say their names...

Balita means 'news'. *Ngayon* means 'now/today'.

Charades with Kuya Resty

Mga bota means 'boots'. *Hindi ko naiintindihan* means 'I don't understand'. When a Filipino tries to communicate in English, but gets stuck on a word and freezes, people around them will say 'nosebleed' and all start to laugh.

On the morning bus...

Kain tayo means 'let's eat'. *Inay* means 'Mother'. *Salo-salo* is a Filipino term that translates as a feast, banquet, party, or reception. It is used to describe the celebration that comes after a wedding, a marriage proposal, or even a job promotion.

Tinikling is a traditional Philippine folk dance which originated during the Spanish colonial era. The dance involves two people beating, tapping, and sliding bamboo poles on the ground and against each other in coordination with one or more dancers who step over and in between the poles in a dance.